Making Their Mark: Women in Science and Medicine™

Margaret Mead
Pioneering Anthropologist

Liza N. Burby

The Rosen Publishing Group's
PowerKids Press™
New York

Published in 1997 by The Rosen Publishing Group, Inc.
29 East 21st Street, New York, NY 10010

First Edition

Book Design: Erin McKenna

Photo Credits: pp. 4, 11 © Corbis-Bettman; p. 7 by Seth Dinnerman; pp. 8, 19 © Archive Photos; pp. 12, 15 © UPI/Corbis-Bettman; p. 16 © AP/Wide World Photos; p. 20 © Charles Rafshoom/Archive Photos.

Burby, Liza N.
    Margaret Mead / by Liza N. Burby
        p.   cm. — (Making their mark)
    Includes index.
    Summary: Discusses the life and work of the noted anthropologist and her accomplishments in the field.
    ISBN 0-8239-5026-3 (library bound)
    1. Mead, Margaret. 1901–1978—Juvenile literature.
    2. Anthropologists—United States—Biography—Juvenile literature.
    [1. Mead, Margaret, 1901–1978. 2. Anthropologists. 3. Women—Biography.] I. Title. II. Series:
Burby, Liza N. Making their mark.
    GN21.M36B87 1996
    306'.092—dc20
    [B]   96–41733
                                                    CIP
                                                       AC

Manufactured in the United States of America

Contents

1	No School for the Mead Children	5
2	A Young Observer	6
3	A Career for Margaret	9
4	Anthropology	10
5	Looking for an Answer	13
6	Changing Anthropology	14
7	A Writer for All People	17
8	Margaret's Favorite Work	18
9	Never Bored	21
10	The Way People See Themselves	22
	Glossary	23
	Index	24

No School for the Mead Children

Margaret Mead was born on December 19, 1901, in Pennsylvania. Her father was a college professor. Her mother was a **sociologist** (so-see-OL-uh-jist). Her grandmother, who lived with them, had been a teacher and a principal. But the Meads did not want their children to go to school. They thought it was better for their children to read books, play outdoors, and use their **imaginations** (im-aj-in-AY-shunz). Margaret's grandmother taught the children at home.

◀ Instead of going to school, Margaret was taught at home, just like these children.

A Young Observer

Grandma Mead believed it was important to look carefully at the world and understand and explain what you saw. Margaret learned from her grandmother to be an **observer** (ob-ZER-ver). What she loved to observe most were people. Margaret played with children of different **ethnic** (ETH-nik) groups. She learned about many different kinds of people.

You can learn a lot from playing with ▶ kids of different backgrounds.

A Career for Margaret

When Margaret was seventeen, she went to college. She was excited by learning new subjects. Margaret always knew she would have a **career** (ka-REER). She began by studying to be a writer. But soon she decided to become a **scientist** (SY-en-tist), because she wanted to learn more about people by studying them.

◀ When Margaret was in college, she was excited about the idea of becoming a scientist.

Anthropology

One day at college Margaret met Franz Boas. He was her **anthropology** (an-throw-POL-uh-jee) professor. Anthropology is an area of science that studies **human beings** (HYOO-man BEE-ingz), how we began and changed, and how we act. Professor Boas believed that by living with groups of people and studying how they act, **anthropologists** (an-throw-POL-uh-jists) can learn new ways to understand humans. Margaret knew from studying with Boas that she wanted to be an anthropologist.

Margaret was very interested in the way other groups of people lived their lives. ▶

Looking for an Answer

Margaret finished college in 1923. She learned that anthropologists did not agree on many things. One important argument was about how people learn. **Nature versus nurture** (NAY-chur VER-siz NUR-cher) are the names for two points of view about this. Some people, like Professor Boas, believe that we nurture, or teach each other how to act. Others believe that we are born to act a certain way. This is called nature. In 1925, Margaret traveled to the islands of American Samoa. By studying the people there, she hoped to learn which point of view was true.

◀ Margaret also studied how different groups of people lived in New Guinea.

Changing Anthropology

In American Samoa, Margaret did many things anthropologists had not done before. She studied women and how they take care of their children. As a woman, Margaret saw the importance of women in **society** (soh-SY-eh-TEE). She also found new ways to get information. For example, she learned the **language** (LANG-widge) of the people she was living with so she could talk with them. What she did there changed the way anthropologists work.

Margaret learned information about mothers and children in New Guinea. ▶

A Writer for All People

When Margaret returned to New York, she told Professor Boas that he had been right. She agreed that people learn their **behavior** (be-HAYV-yor) from others. Margaret wrote a book called *Coming of Age in American Samoa*. This book is for everyone to read, not just for other anthropologists. Margaret thought it was important for everyone to understand what she had learned while living with different groups of people.

◀ Margaret wrote a book on what she learned about nature versus nurture.

Margaret's Favorite Work

Margaret went on many more trips. In the 1930s, her husband, Gregory Bateson, worked with her. Together, they did something that had not been done before. They made movies and took photos of everything they observed. They wanted the rest of the world to see what they saw. This was Margaret's favorite work.

Margaret spoke on the radio and appeared on TV so ▶ everyone could understand what she had learned.

Never Bored

Margaret once said that the thing she was most afraid of was being **bored** (BORD). So she made sure that she always had something interesting to do. She wrote 30 books and many magazine articles. She was a guest speaker on radio and TV, and she gave many talks. She worked at the American Museum of Natural History in New York. She also taught college classes.

◀ Margaret's work at the American Museum of Natural History made her famous.

The Way People See Themselves

Margaret died in 1978. Her work helped many other anthropologists work better. She saw how important women were in their societies. Her work showed the world that people's behavior is formed by what they are taught. Her writing helped people who weren't anthropologists to learn about anthropology and other people around the world.

Glossary

anthropologist (an-throw-POL-uh-jist) A person who studies how humans began and changed and the way they act.

anthropology (an-throw-POL-uh-jee) The study of how humans began and changed and the way they act.

behavior (be-HAYV-yor) How a person acts.

bored (BORD) Not being interested in what you do.

career (ka-REER) A job a person chooses to do.

ethnic (ETH-nik) Members of groups with different skin colors, religions, or cultures.

human being (HYOO-man BEE-ing) Person.

imagination (im-aj-in-AY-shun) Being able to think of new things.

language (LANG-widge) The words people use to speak.

nature versus nurture (NAY-chur VER-siz NUR-cher) Two points of view about how people learn. Nature is the idea that people are born to act a certain way. Nurture is the idea that people teach each other how to act.

observer (ob-ZER-ver) A person who looks at something closely and carefully.

scientist (SY-en-tist) A person who studies the way things are and act in the universe.

society (soh-SY-eh-TEE) People living and working together as a group.

sociologist (so-see-OL-uh-jist) A person who studies groups of people who live together.

Index

A

American Museum
    of Natural
    History, 21
American Samoa,
    13, 14
anthropologists,
    10, 13, 14,
    17, 22
anthropology, 10,
    22

B

behavior, 17, 22
Boas, Franz, 10,
    13, 17

C

*Coming of Age in
    American
    Samoa*, 17

E

ethnic groups, 6

H

human being, 10

I

imagination, 5

L

language, 14

N

nature versus
    nurture, 13

S

science, 10
scientist, 9
society, 14, 22

W

women, study of,
    14, 22
writing, 9, 17,
    21, 22